Recent Titles in
Contributions in Afro-American and African Studies
Series Advisers: John W. Blassingame and Henry Louis Gates., Jr.

The Black Press in the South, 1865-1979
Henry Lewis Suggs, editor

Voices from Under: Black Narrative in Latin America and the Caribbean
William Luis, editor

Contemporary Public Policy Perspectives and Black Americans: Issues in an Era of Retrenchment Politics
Mitchell F. Rice and Woodrow Jones, Jr., editors

Student Culture and Activism in Black South African Universities: The Roots of Resistance
Mokubung O. Nkomo

The Cinema of Ousmane Sembene, A Pioneer of African Film
Françoise Pfaff

Philanthropy and Jim Crow in American Social Science
John H. Stanfield

Israel in the Black American Perspective
Robert G. Weisbord and Richard Kazarian, Jr.

African Culture: The Rhythms of Unity
Molefi Kete Asante and Kariamu Welsh Asante, editor

Writing "Independent" History: African Historiography, 1960-1980
Caroline Neale

More than Drumming: Essays on African and Afro-Latin American Music and Musicians
Irene V. Jackson, editor

More Than Dancing: Essays on Afro-American Music and Musicians
Irene V. Jackson, editor

Sterling A. Brown: Building the Black Aesthetic Tradition
Joanne V. Gabbin

AMALGAMATION!